Fidel Castro
Leader of Cuba's Revolution

Tom Gibb

HODDER
Wayland

an imprint of Hodder Children's Books

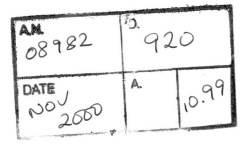
© 2000 White-Thomson Publishing Ltd

Produced for Hodder Wayland by
White-Thomson Publishing Ltd
2/3 St Andrew's Place, Lewes, BN7 1UP

Series editor: Liz Gogerly
Book editor: Cath Senker
Cover design: Jan Sterling, Sterling Associates
Inside design: Joyce Chester
Picture researcher: Shelley Noronha, Glass Onion Pictures
Proofreader: Polly Goodman

Cover picture: Castro speaking to the press after awarding
a medal to athlete Ana Fidelia Quirot, 1995

Published in Great Britain in 2000 by Hodder Wayland, an
imprint of Hodder Children's Books

The right of Tom Gibb to be identified as the author has
been asserted by him in accordance with the Copyright,
Designs and Patents Act, 1988.

A Catalogue record for this book is available from the
British Library.

ISBN: 0 7502 3046 0

Printed and bound in Italy by G. Canale & C.S.p.A.

Hodder Children's Books
A division of Hodder Headline Ltd
338 Euston Road, London NW1 3BH

Picture acknowledgements
The publisher would like to thank the following for giving
permission to use their pictures: AFP 14, 15; AKG 8–9
(both), 11, 18, 21, 22, 34; AP 10, 41, (José Caruci) 42,
(Pool/Paul Hanna) 43; Camera Press 27 (below), 28,
30, 31, 32, 35, 37, 44; Eye Ubiquitous (Leon Schadeberg)
40; Frank Spooner Pictures (Roger-Viollet) 5, (Gamma) 6
(left), (Gamma) 12; HWPL (Cubafotos/John Griffiths) 16,
(T. Morrison) 17, (T. Morrison) 38, (T. Morrison) 45;
Peter Newark Pictures 7, 20, 36; Popperfoto *cover* and *title
page*, 4, 25, 26, 29 (below), 33, 39; Topham Picturepoint
6–7 (centre), 13, 19, 23, 24, 27 (above), 29 (above).

Contents

The Fugitive

It is December 1956. Three ragged fugitives hide from thousands of soldiers in a field of sugar-cane. They have landed in Cuba, part of an 82-strong military expedition. They vow to overthrow the island's brutal dictator, Fulgencio Batista.

But everything goes wrong. They lose their weapons and get lost in swamps. Their guide betrays them to Batista's soldiers.

More than half are killed in a fierce battle or executed afterwards. The rest are scattered. Their leader escapes and hides in the sugar-cane with two followers. Instead of admitting defeat, he whispers excitedly to them: 'We are winning… Victory will be ours!'

'For new generations, the revolution is hardly starting. Those I address today are not the same young men and women of forty years ago. It's different people – but it's the same eternal nation.'
Fidel Castro, 1 January 1999, on the fortieth anniversary of the Cuban revolution.

Opposite **Granma, the boat Castro arrived in, with Castro (left) and Camilo Cienfuegos, one of Castro's military commanders (right).**

Castro in New York, 1955.

4

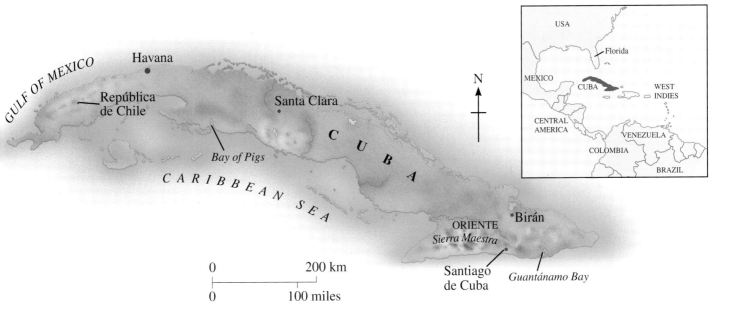

The expedition leader was Fidel Castro. Amazingly, he *did* defeat his enemies. Today, he has held power longer than any other world leader. His enemies call him a tyrant, but his supporters say he is a champion of the poor against the rich countries. With his grey beard and piercing eyes, he is one of the most loved and most hated figures of our age.

Above **Map of Cuba showing the main places that are mentioned in this book.**

Castro's Childhood

Above **Castro (centre), with a brother and sister in Birán, 1929.**

Fidel Castro was born on 13 August 1926 in Birán, eastern Cuba. His father, Angel Castro, was a Spanish soldier who arrived on the island poor. But he was a good businessman and became rich. He started a sugar-cane plantation in the forest and came to employ 500 workers.

Castro had eight brothers and sisters. His mother, Lina Ruz, was the family cook, but became Angel's second wife. When he was small, Castro played with the plantation workers' children.

'I remember Christmases when I was at school. They gave us [about] fifteen days' holiday, starting after December 20th and ending on January 6th, the Day of the Kings. We felt very happy catching the train home. There we had everything: apples, grapes, sweets.'
Fidel Castro.

Right **A man sewing a sack on a sugar-cane plantation in 1948. Such workers received very low pay.**

Right *This American poster from 1947 encouraged rich tourists to visit a large hotel in Havana.*

GAY DAYS UNDER THE CUBAN SUN

Hotel Nacional de Cuba
HAVANA

Right on the shore in Havana, the Nacional stands
in 13 acres of flowering gardens. Two swimming pools,
tennis and many other forms of recreation offer the
winter vacationist the ultimate in luxury.

A Kirkeby Hotel

A corner of the
new Cabana Sun Club...
daily rendezvous of the
smart cosmopolitan set who
revel in Cuba's befalling sunshine

ervations accepted at any of the following Kirkeby Hotels: New York THE GOTHAM • HAMPSHIRE HOUSE • SHERRY-NETHERLAND • THE WARWICK • Philad
WARWICK • Atlantic City THE AMBASSADOR • Chicago THE BLACKSTONE • Upper Saranac Lake, N.Y. SARANAC INN • California BEVERLY WILSHIRE • SUNSE

Nearby, there were much bigger sugar-cane plantations owned by US companies. The Americans lived in large houses with swimming pools. The cane from the Castro farm was turned into sugar at the American-owned mill.

When Castro was five, he was sent to the nearby city of Santiago de Cuba to live with his godfather and a teacher. She was strict and often punished him or threatened to send him to boarding school. One day, Castro realized he would prefer that. So he deliberately broke all the school rules until they sent him there. It was his first rebellion.

Cuba's Fight for Independence

As Castro grew up, he heard many stories about Cuba's independence war (1895–8). For four centuries, the island had been a Spanish colony. But many Cubans wanted freedom from Spanish rule. Castro's father fought on the Spanish side in the independence war.

The Cuban rebels used hit-and-run tactics, hiding among the people. In return, the Spanish moved people into towns, which became like prisons. Hundreds of thousands starved.

An American ship arrives at the port of Havana in 1898, to protect Americans in Cuba.

José Martí, a great thinker and writer, united the Cubans to fight the Spanish. After a long exile, mostly in New York, Martí led a small expedition from Mexico to Cuba. He died in a battle near the beginning of the war, in May 1895. But his ideas still inspire Cubans today.

The Cubans eventually won the war in 1898 when the United States joined them. US battleships sank the entire Spanish fleet. But instead of leaving, the USA then ruled the island for many years. Fidel Castro's father hated the Americans for defeating the Spanish. Cubans who had dreamed of independence also felt betrayed.

'To the battle, Bayameses!
Let the fatherland proudly
observe you!
Do not fear a glorious death,
To die for the fatherland is
to live!'
The song of independence
leaders, now the Cuban
National Anthem.

A portrait of José Martí.

School Days

Castro went to three expensive Catholic schools. He loved sports, and led camping and climbing expeditions. But he fought with the other boys and the teachers.

Castro argued with his father as well. When his father decided to take him away from school, Castro threatened to burn the house down. José Martí became his hero. Castro thought that his father had fought on the wrong side in the independence war against Spain. Also, his father was rich and his workers were extremely poor. Castro believed that this was unfair.

In 1940, when Castro was fourteen, his older half-brother, Pedro Luís, stood against the government in national elections. Pedro offered Castro a horse to get the plantation workers to vote for him. Castro persuaded them to vote for Pedro Luís. But on election day, soldiers arrived and let only government supporters take part anyway. The army had more say in how Cuba was run than the voters.

> '*He succeeded in everything. In sports, in studies. And, every day he would fight. He had a very explosive character.*'
> Raúl Castro about his brother, Fidel, at school.

A rare photo of Castro, as the best athlete of Belén High School in 1945.

Soldiers on the roof of the president's palace in Havana, 1933.

11

Revolutionary Student

Castro studied law at Havana University, from 1945 to 1950. But he spent more time involved in politics. He was an excellent speaker, who captured people's imagination. He joined a political party that wanted to end corruption in Cuba. Sometimes, Castro took a gun to his classes to protect himself from his enemies.

Castro gained a reputation for being wild. Friends say he once drove a bicycle at full speed into a wall, just to prove he could. He led protests against the government at the university.

Castro discussing politics with other students during his time at university.

'If there is one thing I learned throughout those years when I had to look death in the face, unarmed on many occasions, it is that the enemy respects those who do not fear him, those who challenge him.' Fidel Castro.

On 10 March 1952, Fulgencio Batista led an army revolt and took power in Cuba. Batista, a former army sergeant, had ruled Cuba between 1940 and 1944. But he lost the elections in 1944 and again in 1952. So he decided to take power by force instead. Fidel Castro saw his opportunity to start a real revolution. He vowed he would overthrow Batista and began to recruit other students to the struggle.

An army tank in Havana during Batista's army revolt, 1952.

The Moncada Assault

Shortly before dawn on 26 July 1953, Castro led 123
followers in a line of cars towards the Moncada military
barracks in Santiago de Cuba. A thousand soldiers were
asleep inside. Members of Castro's group, including his
younger brother, Raúl, were disguised as soldiers. Most had
hunting rifles and pistols. Castro's idea was to surprise the
soldiers, capture the barracks and declare a revolution.

Castro after his arrest in July 1953, giving evidence to the police.

'**Don't kill them! I order you not to kill them!
I am in command here... You can't kill ideas!**'
Lieutenant Pedro Manuel Sarría, who captured
Fidel Castro's group after the Moncada Assault.

The plan failed. Some of the cars got lost. Shots were fired before most of the rebels were inside the barracks, so most of the soldiers had time to wake up. Castro and his followers fled after killing sixteen soldiers.

Afterwards, the soldiers hunted for the rebels. More than half of them were captured, beaten and shot. Castro was lucky. When he was arrested a few days later, the soldiers wanted to kill him. But the lieutenant in charge stopped them. He did not support Castro, but did not agree with killing prisoners.

Soldiers in Batista's army ready to go into action after the attack on the Moncada barracks by Castro's group.

History Will Prove Me Right

After his arrest, Castro defended himself at his trial with a brilliant speech. He used it to appeal to the nation.

Castro said people should be free to say what they wanted, and to elect their government. He called Batista a miserable tyrant and a *monstrum horrendum* — horrendous monster. He spoke of how unfair it was that many Cubans had no jobs or

A poster made to celebrate the twenty-fourth anniversary of the Moncada Assault.

"XXIV ANIVERSARIO DEL ASALTO AL CUARTEL MONCADA"
LA HISTORIA ME ABSOLVERA HISTORY WILL ABSOLVE ME L'HIST

"El Asalto al Cuartel Moncada, no significo el Triunfo de la Revolución en ese instante, pero señaló el camino y trazó un programa de liberación nacional que abriera a nuestra patria las puertas del socialismo..."

land, yet more than half of the best land was owned by foreigners – mostly by US companies. The Moncada Assault might have failed, he said, but history would prove him right.

Housing in Havana built in the early 20th century, still used today.

At the end of his trial, Castro was sent to prison on an island south of Cuba. He was treated harshly, but was able to write letters from jail telling his followers how to continue the struggle. His speech was published. Soon, everyone in Cuba had heard of him.

'I do not fear prison, just as I do not fear the fury of the miserable tyrant who snuffed life out of seventy brothers of mine. Sentence me, I don't mind. History will absolve me [prove me right].'
Fidel Castro at his trial.

Che Guevara

Castro was freed on 15 May 1955. Batista had just won an election – by cheating – so he felt confident and believed Castro was no longer a threat.

But Castro went to Mexico to recruit followers. He called his group the '26th of July Movement', after the Moncada Assault. He was joined in Mexico by a young Argentinian doctor called Che Guevara.

Vladimir Lenin speaking in Moscow during the revolution that turned Russia into the first Communist country, in 1917.

'If anything good has happened in Cuba since Martí, it is Fidel Castro. He will make the revolution.'
Che Guevara.

Che Guevara (far left) in Argentina in 1948, when he was twenty, photographed with his friends.

In the 1950s, the world was divided between Communist countries allied with the Soviet Union, and capitalist countries allied with the United States. In 1917, the Communists had led a revolution in Russia. The new Communist government took away all private land and set up farms and factories, which it ran itself. The Soviet Union accused the capitalist countries, where people were free to make money, of becoming rich at the expense of poor countries.

Che Guevara openly supported Communist ideas. He said all poor countries should have revolutions. Fidel Castro agreed with some of these ideas, but he only told this to close friends.

The *Granma* Invasion

Castro (centre) with his brother, Raúl (left), and another fighter in the Sierra Maestra mountains, 1957.

'We shall be free or martyrs!' Fidel Castro before the *Granma* Invasion.

In November 1956, Castro left Mexico for Cuba on a motor yacht called *Granma*, which he had bought from an American. Eighty-one followers were crowded on to the decks, including his brother Raúl, and Che Guevara. Castro was following in the footsteps of Martí, who also sailed from Mexico.

Like Martí, Castro planned to unite all Cubans who opposed their rulers. The Communists formed just one group. Others opposed Batista, too, and Castro needed all their help.

The expedition went badly wrong. Ten days later, Castro found himself hiding in a sugar-cane field, most of his followers dead or captured. He and his two companions escaped because local peasants helped them. They brought the rebels food and led them to the mountains of the Sierra Maestra in eastern Cuba. There, Castro met up with Che Guevara, Raúl Castro and nine others, who had also escaped.

Rebels hiding in the mountains of the Sierra Maestra.

Guerrilla War

In the late 1950s, Castro's 26th of July Movement fought a guerrilla war from the Sierra Maestra, where the peasants supported them. The guerrillas made surprise attacks on Batista's soldiers, then quickly hid in the mountains.

Castro led the guerrilla war from the Sierra Maestra.

'The personality of the man is overpowering. It was easy to see that his men adored him... Here was an educated, dedicated fanatic, a man of ideals, of courage and of remarkable qualities of leadership... one got a feeling that he is now invincible [unbeatable].'
Herbert Matthews.

Celia Sanchez (left) and María Hart Santa María, women who were high up in the 26th of July Movement. They are counting money that has been given to the group.

When he had a force of only eighteen men, Castro invited a famous US journalist, Herbert Matthews, to interview him. He told Matthews he had a large, well-armed force. During the interview, a man burst in with a message from the 'second column', which did not really exist. Everyone in the USA and Cuba now heard that Castro had an army in the Sierra Maestra.

One of Castro's greatest helpers was Celia Sanchez. She recruited many poor peasants with promises of land after the revolution. Celia also brought fighters and guns from the cities. She became Castro's lover.

Batista's army was brutal in fighting Castro. Soldiers killed peasants whom they suspected of helping Castro's rebels, and burned down their villages. People started to hate the soldiers and to offer help to Castro.

23

The USA and the War

Castro was not fighting alone. Another group launched an attack on the presidential palace to try to kill Batista. In revenge, the police murdered politicians who were against the government. They arrested, tortured and shot people they thought were helping the rebels.

A protest in about 1958. In 1958–9, Castro's allies organized marches and strikes against Batista's government. These were often brutally crushed by the police.

'When this war is over, I'll start a much longer and bigger war of my own... the war I'm going to fight against them [the United States]. I realize that will be my true destiny.'
Fidel in a letter to Celia, after seeing US rockets destroy a peasant house.

Batista (far right) inspecting a tank that has arrived from the USA. His army relied on arms from the United States.

Large US companies and some Americans supported Batista, because he protected their businesses in Cuba. They were frightened that if the Communists took power, they would lose their businesses. But many Americans became disgusted by Batista's brutality. The USA stopped selling him weapons, but it had already supplied many rockets to Batista's air force.

In public, Castro always said he had no argument with the Americans. He said he would not take land from US companies. Yet in his letters to Celia, he talked of revenge against the Americans.

Batista Flees

Support for Castro's force grew. Castro made his brother Raúl and Che Guevara his main commanders. Many of the rebels had beards, wore scruffy uniforms and were dirty. They had to capture guns from Batista's army. But they fought hard because they believed in their cause. They often beat army forces that were ten times as big as their own. Castro was careful not to kill prisoners, but deserters and spies were executed. Castro learnt to be suspicious of everyone.

Castro talking to rice farmers during his march to Havana, January 1959.

> **'May the monster never return! Honour and glory to the National Hero!'**
> Headlines from *Bohemia*, Cuba's main news magazine, about Castro's defeat of Batista.

Above *Castro's troops, just arrived in Havana from the mountains, being welcomed by thousands of people.* Below *A dove on Castro's shoulder.*

By 1958, almost everyone in the country was against Batista. Guevara won the last big battle, taking the town of Santa Clara in central Cuba. The dictator knew he was defeated and fled the island on 1 January 1959.

A week later, Castro made a triumphant entry into Havana on top of an armoured car. During his first speech as ruler, someone set free some white doves. One landed on Castro's shoulder. Many Cubans believed this to be a sign that he would be a great leader.

Castro's Revolution

After Castro came to power in February 1959, he started to change Cuba. He sent thousands of volunteers to teach peasants to read and write. About 25 per cent of the land was taken away from the rich, including Americans, and given to the poorer peasants. Castro planned to set up free schools and health services – and to give jobs to everyone.

Historians disagree over whether Castro had become a Communist. Some say he was cunning: he knew that if he said he was a Communist, the USA would invade Cuba and overthrow him. This had happened in other Latin American countries. Therefore, when he visited the United States he said he was against Communism. Yet he told the Communists in Cuba he supported them.

Voluntary teachers march in a parade holding giant model pencils. The parade marked the end of a campaign to teach people to read and write.

Above **Cuban schoolgirls going to class at a government school in Havana, 1963.**

Other historians think that Castro wanted to be friendly with the United States. But the USA refused to help. When the Americans stopped trading with Cuba in 1960, Castro was forced to look to the Communist world for help.

'I intend to keep my beard until I have brought good government to my country.'
Fidel Castro on US television, 1959.

Above **Castro shows that he is a man of the people, cutting sugar-cane, 1961.**

Counter-revolutionaries

During 1959, Castro removed his enemies. Guevara led a revolutionary court that executed 550 of Batista's spies and torturers. Castro expelled the man he had himself chosen to be president, Manuel Urrutia. Then he personally arrested a popular commander from his movement, Huber Matos, who opposed the government taking land from private farmers. Castro sentenced him to twenty years in jail. Many people who had fought in the revolution, but were not Communists, were sent to prison or went into exile in Florida, USA. Others who were against Castro also left for the USA.

Right **These Cuban exiles in Florida are doing military training. They are preparing to fight against Castro's government.**

Above **Cuban refugees who went to Florida had to wait in camps like this in Miami until homes were found for them.**

The Florida exiles wanted to overthrow Castro. They had the help of the USA, which did not want a Communist government in the region, even if Cubans supported it. Castro turned to the USSR for weapons. He closed down independent newspapers to stop people criticizing him, and he called his enemies 'counter-revolutionaries'.

However, most Cubans still supported Castro. They agreed with his programmes to provide land, medicine and education for all.

'It is preferable to die rather than turn one's back on the values which animate the cause of truth. History will judge, just as you once said. History will judge you too, Fidel!' Huber Matos.

The Bay of Pigs

On 16 April 1961, US planes flown by Cuban exiles bombed Castro's military headquarters. Castro knew that an exile invasion force, armed and trained by the US spying agency, the Central Intelligence Agency (CIA), was on its way. He thought US troops would invade as well. In a speech to a huge crowd in Havana, Castro declared that Cuba would now be Socialist, allied to the USSR. There would be no more elections.

Cuban peasants doing military training. They are preparing to fight the invasion by Cuban exiles, April 1961.

'This is the Socialist and Democratic Revolution of the humble, with the humble and for the humble.'
Fidel Castro before the Bay of Pigs invasion.

The USA had a military base in Guantánamo Bay in Cuba. Here, US soldiers are doing military exercises in case of war between the USA and Cuba, April 1961.

The exiles landed on a beach called the Bay of Pigs. Castro was told at 3 a.m. and went to oversee the battle.

The exiles had no fighter planes. Cuba had several, including two jets. They sank the invading boats and shot down their supply planes. In the end, the exhausted exiles surrendered. They were eventually returned to the USA for a ransom of $62 million.

In fact, the new young president, John F. Kennedy, had not let US troops take part. He feared this would lead to war with the Soviet Union.

The Cuban Missile Crisis

Castro now became an ally of the USSR. The Soviet Union bought Cuban sugar at high prices. It provided technicians to help Cuban industry. Soviet soldiers and weapons arrived in Cuba, and, in June 1962, the USSR sent nuclear missiles.

A Soviet ship with missiles on board leaves Cuba, November 1962.

'What we affirm is that we must proceed along the path of liberation even if this costs millions of atomic victims.' Che Guevara on the Cuban missile crisis.

Castro in the USSR with Soviet leader, Nikita Khruschev, after the missile crisis.

The idea of Soviet missiles 150 km away from the USA terrified Americans. In October 1962, President Kennedy ordered US warships to surround Cuba and search all Soviet ships to stop more missiles arriving. He threatened to invade unless the USSR took away the missiles. The USSR promised to defend Cuba. The world was at the brink of nuclear war.

Castro wanted the missiles to stay. He believed he could defeat an invasion. But neither the USSR nor the USA wanted to risk a war. They made a deal without Castro. Kennedy promised not to invade Cuba. In return, the Soviet Union took away its missiles. Castro was talking with Guevara when he heard the news. He was furious because he thought he could have got a better deal from the Americans. He swore and smashed a mirror.

Castro's Guerrilla Dream

Castro's dream was to extend his revolution to other countries. In many countries, especially in Latin America, the United States supported brutal military dictators. These rulers were a powerful force against Communism. But they did not allow democracy, and they were greedy and cruel.

A Cuban poster showing Che Guevara on a map of South America. He became a world-wide symbol of guerrilla struggles.

'If we wish to express what we want our children to be, we must say from our very hearts as ardent revolutionaries that we want them to be like Che!'
Fidel Castro in a speech after the death of Che Guevara.

Castro sent Cubans to fight with guerrilla groups in Africa and all over Latin America. Guevara was the real leader of these wars. The CIA tried to catch him many times.

In 1966, Guevara travelled to the mountain rain forests of Bolivia. He believed he could start a revolution that would sweep across Latin America. But the expedition was a disaster. Local Communists did not support Guevara. The following year, he and his followers were caught and executed.

Guevara's death made him a martyr, and an example for guerrillas and freedom fighters worldwide. Castro continued to support groups such as the African National Congress in South Africa, and the Sandinistas in Nicaragua in the 1980s.

Female soldiers from the left-wing Sandinista government in Nicaragua, which Castro helped to overthrow a brutal dictator in 1979. Castro then supported them against right-wing Contra rebels, who were backed by the USA.

El Comandante en Jefe

Since 1959, Castro has ruled Cuba with an iron hand. Generations of Cubans have grown up knowing only him as their leader.

Castro loves to talk. His long speeches are famous, sometimes lasting up to eight hours. He boasts about the achievements of the revolution. Now everyone in Cuba can read and write, and Cubans have a higher ratio of doctors to people than any other country.

Castro is always the centre of attention, a tall, bearded figure in his olive-green uniform. Cubans call him *El Comandante en Jefe* – the Commander-in-Chief. He allows no opposition on the island. Those who criticize him are often arrested, accused of being US-supported traitors. Throughout his rule, hundreds of thousands of Cubans have left the island for the United States. Many have died crossing shark-infested seas on dangerous home-made rafts. Many Cuban families are now split between Cuba and the USA.

A clinic in República de Chile in Cuba. The sign says 'Health is everyone's right'.

'One thing is certain: wherever he may be, however and with whomever, Fidel Castro is there to win. I do not think anyone in this world could be a worse loser.'
Writer Gabriel García Marquez, friend of Castro's.

In 1994, tens of thousands of Cubans fled to Florida on home-made rafts. The refugees in this photo were rescued by US coastguards and taken to the United States.

Cuba Alone

In 1989, the Communist system in the Soviet Union started to collapse. The Cold War between the United States and the Soviet Union was over. For Castro, it was a disaster. The USSR stopped sending aid. Suddenly, Cuba had no one to trade with.

The Cuban exiles believed that Castro would fall too. In 1992, the United States made the economic sanctions – rules against trading with Cuba – even tougher. For a while, there was real hunger in Cuba. In 1994, there was a riot in Havana. Castro went in person to speak to the protesters. Faced with the tall, bearded leader they stopped rioting.

A statue of Lenin being pulled down in Romania, 1990. All the Eastern European Communist governments fell after 1989.

Since 1994, Castro has made some changes. Cuba now trades with Canada and with European countries that disagree with US sanctions. He no longer tries to start revolutions elsewhere. But he remains in charge, and has not changed the political system in Cuba at all.

'Our most sacred duty is to save the Fatherland, the revolution and socialism... The world admires Cuba, and it will admire it even more for our abilities to fight on and win.'
Fidel Castro.

Cuban-American children carrying crosses in memory of people they say were killed by Castro's government.

Castro's Private Life

Alina Fernandez, left, with her daughter, 1997. Alina disagreed with her father's government, and escaped Cuba in 1993 using a fake passport.

While a student, Castro married and had a son, Fidelito, or Little Fidel. But his marriage ended when he fell in love with Naty Revuelta. They wrote passionate letters to each other when Castro was in jail from 1953–55. But Naty did not join Castro's guerrilla struggle in the Sierra Maestra.

With Naty, Castro had a daughter called Alina. When she grew up, Alina argued with her father. She said he always talked but never listened. Alina now lives in Spain.

Castro greeting Pope John Paul II in 1998.

Celia Sanchez, Castro's lover in the Sierra, died of cancer. Since the revolution, Castro has always kept his private life secret. He never married again but is known to have had other children. His son, Fidelito, is now a nuclear scientist.

Castro grew up a Roman Catholic. But after the revolution, he banned public religious worship, and the Christmas holiday. Naturally, the Church criticized Castro. But, recently, he has changed these policies. In 1998, Pope John Paul II visited Cuba. Castro will not say whether he believes in God.

'Worldly appearances should not concern us. All that matters is within ourselves. Despite the miseries of this life there are things that last. There are eternal things, such as my feelings for you, so indelible that they will be with me to the grave.' Castro in a letter from jail to Naty Revuelta.

Castro in History

Castro has seen nine US presidents in office, and says he has survived over 450 murder plots. He still predicts that the USA and capitalism are doomed. Castro believes that Cuba keeps Socialism alive, which is the world's future.

Right *In 1999, Elián Gonzalez survived the shipwreck of a boat taking Cuban refugees to the USA. His US relatives fought to keep him from returning to his father in Cuba. The story showed the terrible divisions in Cuban families.*

Above *Daily life in Cuba: drying rice outside apartment blocks.*

Will history say he was right? Cubans on the island are divided. Some still believe in Castro's brand of Socialism. Others do not. Many are frightened of what will happen when Castro dies and Cuba is left without a strong leader.

Many people in poor countries admire Castro for standing up to the USA for forty years. He helped many freedom fighters who later became popular leaders, such as Nelson Mandela in South Africa. But his enemies say he is a tyrant who will be overthrown one day.

Perhaps people will judge Castro by his last years. Will he and the United States end their conflict? Will he allow change in Cuba? Only Castro knows.

Glossary

armoured car A car with special protection, used in war.

barracks A building used to house soldiers.

Bayameses People of Bayamo, a town in eastern Cuba where one of the first battles of the independence war was fought.

capitalist A capitalist system is one that depends on companies producing goods and making money.

Central Intelligence Agency (CIA) The US government organization that gathers information about how other countries are run, and sometimes gets involved to try to change things.

colony A land run by another country.

Communist Someone who believes in a society where everyone shares things equally. The former Soviet Union called itself Communist.

corruption Using dishonest methods, such as giving people money if they agree to vote for you.

democracy A system of government in which people are allowed to vote for their rulers.

deserters Soldiers who run away from serving in the army.

dictator A ruler who holds total power over a country.

economic sanctions Measures to stop countries from trading with a particular country for political reasons.

exile A person who has had to leave their country.

expedition A journey made for a particular reason.

expelled Threw out.

freedom fighters People who fight against a brutal political system in their country.

fugitive Someone who has run away or had to leave their country.

guerrilla war A war by an independent political group fighting against the country's army.

martyr A person who dies fighting for their beliefs.

military dictator A ruler who holds total power by using the army to keep control.

plantation A large farm.

ransom A sum of money paid in return for the release of a prisoner.

rebellion An organized struggle against the government, or a person not doing as they are told.

recruit To get someone to join an organization.

revenge To harm someone because of something bad they did to you.

surrendered Gave in to the opposing army.

technicians Experts who can apply science to make things work, such as machines for industry.

traitors People who do things that harm their own country.

tyrant A cruel ruler.

Date Chart

1898 Cuban victory against the Spanish. US rule begins.

1926, 13 August Fidel Castro is born in Birán, eastern Cuba.

1945–50 Fidel goes to Havana University.

1952 Fulgencio Batista takes power.

1953, 26 July Fidel leads the Moncada Assault.

1955, 15 May Castro is freed from prison and goes to Mexico to recruit followers.

1956, November Fidel and eighty-one followers leave Mexico on the motor yacht *Granma*. Castro leads a guerrilla war in the Sierra Maestra mountains.

1959, 1 January Batista flees.

1959, February Castro becomes the ruler of Cuba and removes his enemies.

1960 The USA stops trading with Cuba.

1961, 16 April Cuban exiles invade Cuba, in the Bay of Pigs invasion.

1962, June The USSR sends nuclear missiles to defend Cuba, leading to the Cuban missile crisis.

1966 Che Guevara and his followers go to Bolivia to start a revolution.

1967 Guevara and followers are killed.

1980s Castro supports freedom fighters in other countries, such as the ANC in South Africa.

1989 The Communist system in the USSR starts to collapse.

1994 Riots against the government in Havana.

1998 Pope John Paul II visits Cuba.

Further Information

Books to Read
Country Insights: Cuba by Marion and Tony Morrison (Wayland, 1997)

Heinemann Profiles: Fidel Castro by Petra Press (Heinemann, 2000)

Websites
http://library.thinkquest.org/18355/
The Cuban experience – Cuban culture, history and politics – including Castro

http://www.abcnews.go.com/reference/bios/castro.html
ABC is one of the major US TV channels – this is put up by ABC, and has useful links to other good sites to help you find out more about Castro.

Video
Biography: Fidel Castro. A documentary about Castro's life.

Index

Page numbers in **bold** mean there is a picture on the page.